BALLOONING IN STARS

Matthew Edward Schatmeyer

Gotham Books

30 N Gould St.
Ste. 20820, Sheridan, WY 82801
https://gothambooksinc.com/

Phone: 1 (307) 464-7800

© 2023 *Matthew Edward Schatmeyer*. All rights reserved.

No part of this book may be reproduced, stored in a retrieval system, or transmitted by any means without the written permission of the author.

Published by Gotham Books (December 1, 2023)

ISBN: 979-8-88775-270-9 (P)
ISBN: 979-8-88775-272-3 (H)
ISBN: 979-8-88775-271-6 (E)

Because of the dynamic nature of the Internet, any web addresses or links contained in this book may have changed since publication and may no longer be valid.

The views expressed in this work are solely those of the author and do not necessarily reflect the views of the publisher, and the publisher hereby disclaims any responsibility for them.

Table of Contents

CHAPTER ONE: NATURAL BEAUTY (LIFTOFF)

Alongside

Ballooning

Chrysalis

Color of Time

Dew

Greening (come Spring)

Impulse

In stars

Morning

Of colors and hues...

Pinpricks

Prism

Rainbow Soul

Sailing

See Change (about time)

Silica Souls

Slow waves (breaking)

Spreading...

Starlight

Stone's Throw (reflection)

CHAPTER TWO: SHARED EXPERIENCE (SOARING)

About Reality

Being (human)

Caress

Clearing

Destiny's Dream (waiting)

Doublespeak

Do you think of me when it rains?

First and Foremost

Golden Grace

Gravity

HumansPeak

Laughing (underwater)

Love is...

Mirrors

Pals Forever

Promises Unveiled

Reciprocity

Reunion (never apart)

Same as me

Sunlit sky (out of the blue)

Tears

Unbreakable

Underneath (tile or grass)

Understanding...

CHAPTER THREE: INSIDE OURSELVES (FLIGHT)

Apart
Awakening Beauty
Because (coins)
Black Backdrop
Bring yourself...
By a nose (for Rose Time)
Daydream
Dream a day away (for Will)
Given Time
Heart (felt)
Imperfections
Juggler
Learning to Live (this day)
Letting go (soaring)
Never full of emptiness
Pathways
Pegasus
Rolling Dice (sides)
Second Try (solitaire)
Sudden Spring
Sunset (without regret)
Swingsetting
Thaw
Time to Shine (candles)
Town Whistle
Two of Hearts
Waterfalling

———————————— ✦ ————————————

CHAPTER FOUR: FOREVER FORWARD (TOUCHDOWN)

any Given day (sandcastles)

Eternity never fades away

Hymn to ourselves

Inception (emergence)

Indian Summer

Journeying

Remembrance (rain & sun)

Rivers

Structure

Through Heaven's Gate (transformation)

Tremendous Love

Waves (coming Home)

————————————✦————————————

NATURAL BEAUTY (LIFTOFF)

ALONGSIDE

Angels ever after
push us onward
with their wingbeatings,
guiding us alongside.
Their breath filling our slack sails,
we're no longer aimless nor adrift.
Out of the wonderful, terrible
expanse of a boundless ocean
we're heading toward
the same Horizon.
Alongside one another.
Our wake is
a wake…
splashing turquoise truth
onto a
laughing porpoise tooth!

BALLOONING

Every body that houses a Soul
has a different form.
Some are as jet planes,
supersonic in transit
just to sit
on the tarmac.
Some are more like iron trains,
lumbering along without wit
just to stay
on the track.
We are colorful airships.
Our ballast?
In a bottle, a vial, a vile bottle.
The only way to control our flight
is the height of our emotions.
Rise and fall, we do.
That's all we can do.
Winds will take us where they may…
different winds at each altitude
That's how you steer a hot air balloon.
Lost in the clouds… too high!
Fall toward the mire… too low!
Sandbags of salt, so we don't fly away.
Warm words needed to coast over mountains.
I ask Jesus, please
lift me to The breeze
that will land me softly
in God's Forever field.
Carry me home to Heaven.

CHRYSALIS

Butterflies
change themselves.
They crawl to nibble leaves.
They don't appear lovely,
they look like spiny worms.
They are still butterflies,
Inside...
Full, they sleep
where they feel safe,
encased outside of time.
They are still butterflies,
Inside...
Then a magical sunray warms the chrysalis
until the dawning moment
of their most beautiful rebirth!
Bursting forth amongst
the vales, meadows, gullies, brooks, and becks.
A multitude of shimmering splendor!
Every one unique,
especially these two...
one silver and one gold.

COLOR OF TIME

As I peer into
days passed
I see them as...
emotion hued
and imbued
with colors.
Time is woven as fine fabric
making up the patchwork pattern
that shows all of our colors
to be the same.

Dew

is a cloud
on the grass.
See them high,
feel them low,
between toes.
No two clouds
ever the same
in our sky.
Dew is all the same
upon this field...
our common ground.

Greening (come Spring)

As the waking world warms
from its quiet pause,
blossoms become substance
instead of a frozen dream.
They need rain,
they need air,
they need sunshine!
That is all that
they need.
We are neither plants nor animals,
we are humans with splendid Souls.
We need kind words,
we need passion,
we need togetherness,
we need honesty.
We need love...
to flourish,
to bring our lives meaning.
We need one another
                to join in this greening.

IMPULSE

A lightning bolt,
the shadow of a perfect eclipse,
or a supernova star...
exist only as an impulse.
Living and leaving
at the same moment in Time.

IN STARS

Inside ourselves
reside energies
that will last Forever.
To build,
to change
tomorrow.
In stars...
inside

Morning

storm clouds are beautifully risen.
Back and forth they waver,
just waiting for the sun and the wind
to mold them.
To bring forth roses or floods.
Eventually?
Both...

OF COLORS AND HUES...

The wind tears through the trees tonight.
She tugs at the front door.
Proud pine and aspen burn before me.
Living and dying.
Changing hue.
Red to orange to blue
like the eyes of a girl I once knew.
Onyx startles me
from this reverie
his sleek, black head nudges my knee
affectionately.
He loves to nibble earlobes
so I let him
even though it tickles.
His eyes are emerald green,
a color like I've never seen...

PINPRICKS

Looking outward into
the jet-black depths that
seem to go on forever...
just space
with nothing waiting
to be made into newer Nothingness.
Touch a star...
if you can!

PRISM

Inside every heart
is a prism that reflects
all of the colored emotions
that make our souls unique.
When the sun is just right,
Yellow white...
I feel Forever

Rainbow Soul

Rainbows follow rain, but not always...
that's what I always say!
There's no other way
to see the multicolored hue
that is you...
until after the storm has passed, it's true!
We all climb mountains in our own manner...
no gold stars, no blue ribbons.
Your life's tapestry your only proud banner,
a simple gratitude, taken and given.
The sky's the limit!
Cobalt blue never ending...
except for the clouds within it.
My well-worn soul's like
a roof that needs mending.
The rain can't go on forever!
In my true heart's a treasure.
Knowledge that this tumultuous storm,
confusing, chaotic, without coherent form...
only feels like a cataclysm,
then becomes a focusing prism!
Within life's lens, a moment's still frame.
Thank God... no two rainbows ever appear the same!

SAILING

ships are made of wood.
If we could
make a sailing ship of
purest gold?
It would
sink to
become a
treasure only...

See Change (About Time)

That cloud billowing high
into a fine summer sky
caught my eye.
Only to look away
for the briefest moment
to look back and see...
it will never
appear the same to me.
A chance to glance
at a sunlit flower
dewy from this
passing thundershower.
Only to look away
for a thousand heartbeatings
to look back and see
an older Sun fleeting.
As its petals close
it will never
appear the same to me.
Now, I'm alone in the dusk
to find the first star
so very far from where we are.
I'll watch it for
three billion heartbeats...
it will always
appear the same to me.
Yet, I'm changing.
More than the star,
less than the cloud,
a little like the flower.
As the moon rose...
she reversed the tide of my soul.
All this, in less than an hour

Silica Souls

our Souls are pebbles
in a stream
that we call Time...
Buffeted this way and that,
currents affecting where we rest.
Cold eddies circle the pebble,
protected, but going nowhere new,
just wearing the layers away...
Warm swell buoys the stone,
absorbing the sun's warmth so true,
expanding the layers that may.
Descending rapids let it go,
fallen and fissured,
a pebble in a pile,
content to let layers decay.
Until we're all sand together
to be melted and made
into the flawless glass window
that only God sees through.
Pick up a pebble, knowing
that it is a grain of sand.

Slow Waves (Breaking)

Solid sun
warms the air
to make the winds
that make the waves.
Starting somewhere,
each one does,
to end up
slowly breaking,
to end up
where it was
meant to be all along.

Spreading...

as sunshine does over
freshly fallen snow,
reflected thoughts
mirrored within a million diamonds,
One day melting
into a stream...
to be forgotten.

STARLIGHT

From a billion years past,
another sun's spark
filters down at last.
I am not afraid
to be happy
anymore…

Stone's Throw (reflection)

Pitch a pebble into a quiet pond...
and the ripples spread to the shore
slowly, never quite still. Still.
Toss a heavy rock into a fast moving river...
and it disappears
rapidly, only churning current behind it. It.
Bump a boulder into the ocean...
becoming, as if it never happened. Happened.
I am not the pebble, but the pond.
I can not be the river, nor the ocean.
Flow slow to reflect. Reflect.

SHARED EXPERIENCE (SOARING)

About Reality

About one half of Reality
is Definition.
About one half of Reality
is Perception.
How does each one of us
define Reality?
Through OUR Perception...

Being (human)

At times we all feel as if...
every plastic clocktick
stretches like taffy
that is not sweet.
Imprisoned within time.
At times we all feel as if...
every liquid sunbeam
flows like love
that is beyond sweet.
Released from time.

CARESS

To be human...
is to understand
just how little time
that we have to
touch one another.
There are many
different ways to
reach out
to be human...
Shake a hand,
rub a shoulder,
pat a back,
hug a chest to your own,
to be human...
None like kissing you
as I look into those soft eyes...
not wanting to turn off the lamp,
knowing that I must
let myself fall
into the sweet caress
of together sleep.
To be humans...

CLEARING

Once upon a time, there stood a forest on the edge of imagination. Truly, two forests separated by a clearing between. On the one side lived Mandarin. He had lived all his life amongst the grey, withered trees on the northern side. He knew only that it was his duty to patrol the craggy, sad branches and scrubby bushes. He carried his rifle as he paced endlessly. Taking aim at the occasional crow but mainly, specifically, looking for yellow-eyed wolves. He knew not why nor what he was protecting from them. He just felt that there must be somewhere that light shone, somewhere that he had never visited. Oh, he had heard tales but he never really believed them. He just shot the wolves. He lived on soup made from the bitter-tasting bark of the dark forest that surrounded him. He had a lot of time to think during his patrols, just not much to think about.

At the same moment in time, Sapphire plucked ripe fruit from the sunny, green orchards near the southern end of this forest of the imagination. She spent her days going from splendid tree to splendid tree, gathering all that she could into her basket. Looking for the freshest fruit to make wonderful pies, and the occasional batch of sweet-tasting cider. She knew not why nor what she did, only that she loved to make tasty treats. She just felt that there must be somewhere that was not so sunny, and bright all the time. Oh, she had heard tales but she never really believed them. She just picked the fruit. She lived on something like applesauce that was made from the fruit of the sunlit orchards that surrounded her. She had a lot of time to think during her picking, just not much to think about.

One day, Mandarin could find no wolves to slay in his part of the forest. He traveled farther and farther southward, thinking that maybe he had finally shot all of the wood's evil beasts! This same day, Sapphire could find no fruit to pick in her part of the forest. She traveled farther and farther northward, thinking that maybe she had finally picked all of the orchard's good fulfillments!

Before them both stood a clearing, vacant of trees, yet full of sun and shadows. The sunbeams and the dimness spun together to meet in the center... as in the eye of a wonderful, terrible hurricane. Timidly, Mandarin and Sapphire both advanced a step forward, then another. Seeing each other, they began to move more boldly ahead. Meeting in the middle, in a swirling whirlwind of all that has ever been or will be... they had no choice but to embrace.

From this day on, the world was brought into balance. An equality of light, terror, dark, and bliss. Real love was born as loneliness disappeared, in this forest clearing... with a very special kiss!

Destiny's Dream (Waiting)

A whole lifetime of hope
within each of our hearts.
Realized in a heartbeat.
Did you invent me
into your dream?
Lasting love found.
Have I always been here
waiting only for you?
To spend Forever together...

Doublespeak

Folly, fault, forgive...
to talk through tin cans that
humble humans hold.
Severed string silences
any and all attempts at
considerate communication...

Do you think of me when it rains?

Do you think of me when it rains,
as soft thunder rattles the windowpanes?
Acute sadness throbs in every vein.
Will it always be the same?
Grey tide scours the world clean,
leaves me feeling empty.
Ceaseless pounding, bludgeoning and mean.
Oh, can't you help me?
Slate clouds send a cold story in Morse,
mixing, running with a fool's salty tears.
Thoughts of remorse follow their course.
Will I always carry these same old fears?
Always you will remain my nectar and my bane,
a world of love, tinged with pain.
Who can say now who's to blame?
Tell me though… do you think of me when it rains?

First and Foremost

Please
and
I'm sorry.
Use these words often...
Thank you!

Golden Grace

The Golden Rule?
Solid as the same metal.
Yet, every shining sunbeam
spreads a shadow.
In that shadow?
We do unto others
what has been done unto us.
In the light?
We remember to
do unto others
as we would have done unto us.
Stay in the sunlight!

GRAVITY

Inexorable, this gentle tug,
inescapable, joined in
harmonious balance.
Locked in
tide and time
spinning through aeons.
Paired and partnered,
bound to be...
as one.
A comet's icy trail
hangs as God's etching
in the heavens.
Shimmering sky,
thickening air...
so still.
Listen as the leaf
stops spinning...
as the first drop falls.
All these years
pulling down.
As the sky sheds its burden?
We may as well...

HUMANSPEAK

There are times when it is best to…
say nothing.
Times when you must…
say something.
Times when you have to…
say everything.
Anytime?
Say ' I love you! '

Laughing (Underwater)

You and I share
our secrets
as if
we were in open air.
Only we know...
that it feels
more like
laughing underwater!

LOVE IS...

stronger than anger.
Ultimately...
all that you own
is your own Love.
Anger owns you.
When you share your Love?
You will find more.
More than before...
more than you thought

Mirrors

Only one you,
only one me.
We look inside to see our
infinitely reflected energy.
We take the good with the bad,
it's all to be had...
as light and love play
funhouse tricks
on our hearts and minds.
Figure out what's real,
and what's left in the shadows.
Then talk to me,
as humans ought to.
To this day...
what brought you?
There are no two mirrors nor souls
made by man or God,
in the entire world
exactly the same.
Not a single one

Pals Forever

We know what it means
to really care.
If one of us leans
the other is right there!
It may have been a call
from a lonely mountaintop.
Or a temporary stall
then a ride to help my Pop!
A card or a gift
aren't enough, not all that I need to say.
How special it is that we lift
our spirits throughout each day!
On this Father's Day I give
all my love and respect to you.
Fine friendship is our treasure…
one without measure!

P‍romises U‍nveiled

A spectrum shown
within every promise...
Falsities
Assistances
Hopes
Foundations
Truths
Friendships
Loves
Forever

RECIPROCITY

What you put in,
what you get back?
Works only for math equations
and cake recipes,
rarely for relationships ..

REUNION (NEVER APART)

We've made it through,
together.
We've created today to be what it is,
together.
We've built an unshakeable pact of love,
together.
You are altogether...
my best friend!

Same as Me

You're the same as me,
golden child of God.
Filled with spirit and gentle compassion.
Spilling warmth as you laugh eagerly.
Without care, never a doubt.
Within care, kindness flowing out.
Enveloping all, as the moon's full tide.
Content in your skin, along for the ride.
Quick with your wit, even quicker to smile.
Coasting aloft, like sun-drenched clouds adrifting.
Unblemished by the callous world, innocent child.
Fragile, whole as you are... something is missing.
The companion, the kindred soul that you lack?
To confide in, to trust, to befriend.
Someone as deep, mirrored pond looking back?
Someone who feels, not just pretends.
Your eyes, your thoughts, are a calm tranquil sea.
Let me know them.
Only then will our love be
gathered like ripe fruit on a tree,
as we find out... you're the same as me!

Sunlit Sky (Out of the Blue)

In your eyes
of truest blue...
I see beyond,
into Forevertime.
As I hold your hand,
you should know...
I feel beyond,
into Forevertime.
Faded jeans,
sun on the waters,
sparkling sapphires,
skies without limits...
As we laugh,
as we share
ourselves together...
I wonder if you really know?
How we do,
how we always have,
how we always will...
share the same soul
of deepest blue!

Tears

Tears form tears
that rip us apart,
separate us.
Just words,
not swords.
Cleave and leave?
Or sit in the sun and share?
Brooks talk as
waterfalls shout and
rivers renew!

UNBREAKABLE

Brittle branches can't bend.
Hard hearts won't mend.
Ours always do!
I'm human,
just like you...

Underneath (tile or grass)

It doesn't matter much
what you are standing on,
as much as
who you are standing with.
I won't walk away from you...
even if you tell me to!

Understanding...

that yesterday means nothing,
that today means something,
that tomorrow
means everything!
Does not mean anything
unless we care...
I'll meet you there.

INSIDE OURSELVES (FLIGHT)

APART

from yesterday,
from tomorrow.
Apart from the man in the next lane in his Volvo
who lost his dog and has asthma.
A gulf,
a sequence of worlds between.
Oh God, please do not let me come apart...

Awakening Beauty

How can it be
that within the ocean of your
closed cornflower blue eyes
swim demons of doubt?
Wake up to my honest love
as you let me put your
restless heart to sleep…
kissing you from deep within
then awakening you
to our together tomorrow

Because (coins)

you chose to love me?
I love you.
you understand me?
I know you.
you forgive flawed me?
I cherish you.
Worn coins do
hold greater value!
Let us make a wish
as we toss ours
into the deep well
of our dreams

BLACK BACKDROP

Against it,
we were.
Together,
so sure!
Nothing between,
so it did seem...
two stars bound,
motion in parallel.
Meteoric love found
as we fell

BRING YOURSELF...

to a boil, trying not to
burn yourself with the passion of youth.
Spill all of the rice
onto the smooth countertop
that is the world.
Pick out which grain is YOU!
Think about the potentiality,
the possibility that you
have the inspiration
to be different,
to be separate
from the rest of the rice.
Put that grain into the simmerpot first.
To find out later...
that you are just like the rest of the rice.
Uniquely a part, not apart!

By a nose (for Rose Time)

Life is like a horse race,
know your place,
keep your pace,
give it all to show your grace!
All we can do, I suppose…
is to hope for Rose,
that she may win by a nose!

Daydream

I'll find us a place
to sit in the sun.
That's what I'll do!
I'll do it for me,
I'll do it for you.
Dreaming...
temple on warm bark,
about thousands of tomorrows

Dream a Day Away (for Will)

Cleated shoes shuffle in the sand.
Iron doughnuts swung on bats stretch muscles
in the on deck circles...
each one waiting for their chance
to swing for the fences.
A Home Run!
That's all I need to do
to win the game,
to be the best!
To be the star,
to be the hero!
I see that ball sailing high
in my mind's eye...
carrying on a fortunate breeze,
floating, rising with effortless ease.
The delayed crack of a sweetspot smack
resonating toward my adoring fans.
Higher and higher fly the leather and clothbound seams,
never stopping... this perfect flight!
The stuff of dreams,
knocked that ball clear out of sight!
A lazy curveball on a lazy day
by a lazy pitcher...
I got my way!
Smashed it, turning hips with all my might,
knocked that softie pitch clear out of sight!
I see it lofting, lost against
a clear bright blue sky...
over the diamond wire fence!
I open my eyes...
and step up to the plate.
The third base coach
rubs his elbow...

NO!
I want to swing away!
I want to be the champion!
I saw it happen
crystalline clear!
The sign meant bunt,
the catcher bobbled the ball
and Timothy made it to third base.
Digging hard,
I made it to first.
I did make it Home that daydream afternoon
to score the winning run,
not because I smashed it out of the park...
WE won
because I listened...
to lay down the perfect bunt!

GIVEN TIME

No givin' up,
no givin' in!
Never settle,
because then
you can't win!
Try, and
try again!
The devil's song is apathy
and I'm not listenin'!
It's givin' time...

Heart (felt)

Let yourself be touched.
Place your own hand
over your own heart
and you can't feel its beat.
You can see it above your inside heel.
Not so odd, by God…
takes others to feel!

IMPERFECTIONS

make us real to
one another.
Pets, friends, lovers, family...
all flawed perfectly.
I have beautiful birthmarks.
I am imperfect.
I love...

JUGGLER

To find a steady mind
that can balance
emotions is hard for all of us to do...
on a tightrope too!
Let some balls fall.
Not your heart, though!
It's a long way down...

Learning to Live (This Day)

I had to disassemble myself,
to be shattered,
to put a new self back together,
piece by painstaking piece.
To become whole again.
To finally say on this day
that I know what it means
to forgive and love myself.
Everything to do with our true hearts
has happened for a reason.
Our together tears
cementing us like glue.
I am so glad to be alive,
so proud to be imperfectly human,
so thankful for the simple love of true friendship,
as we hold each other close.
I had no idea how much love we carry inside
until I stopped running away
and started learning to live.

LETTING GO (SOARING)

The hardest
thing
that we as
humble
humans
have
to do is
to let go of...
Anger
Pain
Guilt
Comfort
sometimes even Love
Then eventually?
Let go of ourselves
to soar Heavenward ^o^

Never full of emptiness

A pen, then a pillow
are all I need tonight.
Still though
it will take all my might...
to make certain tomorrow
will never feel this hollow

PATHWAYS

I chose to stay…
Unscarred,
yet I'm not.
In love,
but I couldn't.
Resentful,
just not for long.
Hopeful,
and I did!
Myself ?
Forever…

PEGASUS

Holding fast
onto my pretty pony
of Hope and Beauty...
of Tenderness.
Careful in the saddle,
not to be
Proud nor Discouraged.
Spreading wide Wings
to leave those muddled muddy worries
far below to
fly into the sky of Promise!

Rolling Dice (sides)

One is none.
Two's a silver coin.
Four is an emerald pyramid.
Six is a ruby square
seen everywhere.
Eight is a shining sapphire.
Ten's a clear diamond.
Hundred is a golden chance.
NEVER could there be
a die with sides of three!
May be in Heaven...

Second Try (solitaire)

I did it!
I have done nothing...
I won!
I am lost...
Played out perfectly!
To fall into disarray...
alternating orderly rows!
Chaos and chance...
Hinging on the last card!
Never be the one...
to finish and be done!
It's just too hard...
To you? Today?
May not matter...
our ashes will scatter.
To me? Tonight?
Means everything...
swear I heard the angels sing
when I found the King...
Hope and Heaven,
toil and turmoil...
within myself,
not fifty-two from Hoyle!

Sudden Spring

You
brought forth a
sudden Spring
into my coldest Winter.
You
deserve more
thank you's than
I have words for.
Sudden Spring so sunlit!

Sunset (without regret)

Finding our way
through...
through each day that
may...
may end in dismay.
Try...
try though to find
every...
every sunset to be
one...
one without regret!

SWING SETTING

Push me gently
and often,
please.
Rhythmic resonance
rising repeatedly as we
reach inside to
reach out.
I guess this is what they call Love!
Steady me as I return
from touching the sky
to touch you

THAW

To the one who helped me to remember,
when I was stranded upon a sea of dark possibility...
called me forth from frozen
remote solitude, that perpetual December.
Sadness pervaded my world, so unwanted.
In a deep hole I'm swallowed
by dismay and tragedy, I'm haunted.
Where is the path that I am to follow?
The brilliant sunshine of your smile
turned me back toward the light
and the love that has become such a
welcome warmth.

Time to Shine (candles)

I thought that I was burning bright,
my duty to make everything right.
Just burning, churning, and yearning
for the day of my returning.
To myself.
It felt like a chasm, with me in the center.
Forgotten my heart, and what it was meant for.
To share myself.
Reflected from you,
my light a dim candle.
In the mirror of our openness,
I saw half a lifetime askew.
All by myself.
Please be my friend,
that's all I ever wanted.
As I begin to mend,
to continue undaunted.
Knowing myself.
It's my time to shine,
it's your time to shine.
Let us ignite love within the other,
to divine life's riddle.
Shall we each…
share our light a little?
That we may…
melt in the middle!
Becoming ourselves.

TOWN WHISTLE

At high noon,
like clockwork.
Only mine says 12:05.
No two ever view
the world
in quite the same way!
Wound up
to unwind.
To pass the time...

Two of Hearts

I shuffled my life
like a deck of cards.
Until,
I found that you can't play this game
missing one...

WATERFALLING

Dam them up
from sunup to sundown,
against tidal push,
for far too long.
How have you held back
the river of your emotions?
Let them go,
let them show,
let them flow.
Let your fears
spill over into
calmer waters...

FOREVER FORWARD (TOUCHDOWN)

Any Given day (sandcastles)

Any given day
is a gift from God.
A chance to understand that…
you are,
and you will be,
a single grain of sand
on the shores of Heaven.
To do mighty things,
breaking a wave's progress.
To do wonderful things,
forming part of a child's fortress.
To do dreamy things,
holding still lovers' footprints.
To do kind things,
sheltering a clam's home.
Since…
a grain of sand
is not a shore,
and a lone feather
is not a pair of wings…
Only Together,
may we do such beautiful things!

Eternity never fades away

Eternity will never fade away.
Our short season here?
A little every day...
like an ice cream cone
melting in late May.
How sweet life is!

Hymn to Ourselves

People are all that matter this side of Heaven.
Any emotion of duration ought to
be rooted in tolerance and forgiveness.
God's honest Truth...
Believe that!

Inception (Emergence)

Womb to warmth to worry to wisdom.
Lives led as a preciously precarious picture
already drawn by the careful Hand of God.
Since your inception…
the lullaby
remembered
deepdown,
remains part of you…
until its emergence
as the simply splendid song
that is yours alone.
To join in the chorus…
that is our harmoniously
rising rhythm
carrying to God.

Indian Summer

Sometimes your tooth hurts
or you skin a knee...
beyond this, we shall be.
Sometimes it is warm and pleasant
or cold and sleeting...
beyond this, we shall be.
Sometimes there is loss and void
or we are filled with contentment...
beyond this, we shall be.
I did see the Promise of Beyond on an early summer day
to a Place of such unadorned and miraculous Peace.
I glimpsed a Perfect horizon
with a Sun never quite setting.
I asked to be Saved for all time,
and God remembered me.
Beyond this, we shall Be!

JOURNEYING

Sweet souls...
let us thank ourselves,
for it is a long road to Glory.
As long as we have a full tank of Love,
we can always help one another to fix a flat tire.
There is no starting line
nor a finish line to cross.
This well trodden Way
stretches to Eternity.
Gentle men and women
start your engines...

Remembrance (Rain & Sun)

Words and thoughts
comprise us.
They make us who we are.
In the Spanish tongue?
Llueve is both rain and cry.
Sonrisa is both sunrise and smile.
Spread your palm to the sky,
or place it over your humble heart
as you speak these words.
To show whether God is crying,
or your own human eyes are shedding tears.
As you let be known whether God's smile brings a new day,
or your own human soul welcomes another with warmth.
Let us…
feel every raindrop as His tear,
remember every sunrise as His smile.

Rivers

all empty into the sea.
They all flow fluidly to
find their way there.
Gravity is like love.
I hope that we all do
follow our courses to...
all fill this sea
that is called
Togetherness

STRUCTURE

There is only One
True Architect.
God Himself.
He lays down
His Plan.
For us.
Sent His Son
to be our Carpenter.
To build this Love?
Each day IS a brick...

Through Heaven's Gate (Transformation)

All of my worries
Forever disappearing...
as the Love of a very real God
floods into the core of my being.
He remembers me
when I forget myself.
His Son's Sacrifice
makes all possible.
A serene Peace
for all of us
for all Eternity

Tremendous Love

Within my quiet soul,
in a place I didn't quite know,
lay a dormant truth in the dark.
I was forlorn and dismal.
Then with a lovely, caring spark,
light and love rescued me from the abysmal.
Open doors, open minds, open hearts,
still... all too soon,
we must depart.
I'll never forget the warmth
shown to me in kindness' hearth.
The most gentle creatures I've met on this Earth,
special friends... all of you!
Let us welcome our Rebirth.
A more wonderful time could only be found in Heaven above,
than to give and be given this tremendous love

Waves (coming Home)

Onto the shores of Heaven,
we're just waves...
coming Home

(never) the end

I thank you, Kind Reader…

For sharing this time together.

My Mother, Sherrey Ann Welch,
always 'cheered me on',
always 'cheered me UP!'
Allove Forever^

About the Author

Matthew Edward Schatmeyer currently resides in Sterling Heights, Michigan, U.S. of A.

This lifelong bachelor's passions include reading, writing, and classic automobiles.

Fluent firstmost in 'Feline', followed by 'Latin', thirdly in 'Dragon'…and is learning 'English'.

www.ingramcontent.com/pod-product-compliance
Lightning Source LLC
LaVergne TN
LVHW061625070526
838199LV00070B/6582